RESEARCH TOOLS FOR THE CLASSICS

American Philological Association Pamphlets

Research Tools for the Classics

The Report of the American Philological Association's Ad Hoc
Committee on Basic Research Tools

John F. Oates, Chair

Edited by
Roger S. Bagnall

Number 6

RESEARCH TOOLS FOR THE CLASSICS

THE REPORT OF THE
AMERICAN PHILOLOGICAL ASSOCIATION'S
AD HOC COMMITTEE ON BASIC RESEARCH TOOLS

edited by

Roger S. Bagnall

SCHOLARS PRESS

Distributed by
Scholars Press
101 Salem Street
Chico, California 95926

Research Tools for the Classics

edited by
Roger S. Bagnall

copyright ©1980
American Philological Association

Library of Congress Cataloging in Publication Data

American Philological Association. Ad Hoc Committee on
  Basic Research Tools.
  Research tools for the classics.

  (American Philological Association pamphlets ; no. 6)
  Bibliography: p.
  1. Classical languages--Study and teaching.
2. Reference books--Classical philology. I. Bagnall, Roger S.
II. Title. III. Series: American Philological Association
American Philological Association pamphlets ; no. 6.
PA76.A65 1981   480'.07   80-25766
ISBN 0-89130-452-5 (pbk.)

Printed in the United States of America
1   2   3   4   5
Edwards Brothers, Inc.
Ann Arbor, Michigan 48106

CONTENTS

THE AD HOC COMMITTEE ON BASIC RESEARCH TOOLS

John F. Oates, Chairman, Duke University

Roger S. Bagnall, Columbia University

G.W. Bowersock, Institute for Advanced Study

Henry M. Hoenigswald, University of Pennsylvania

W. Robert Connor, Princeton University

Philip Levine, University of California at Los Angeles

Elaine Fantham, Trinity College, University of Toronto

John J. Bateman, University of Illinois, Urbana

Ronald Stroud, University of California at Berkeley

William E. Metcalf, American Numismatic Society

Claireve Grandjouan, Hunter College, CUNY

Bernard Knox, Center for Hellenic Studies, Washington

Alexander P.D. Mourelatos, University of Texas, Austin

LIST OF ABBREVIATIONS

ACLS   American Council of Learned Societies

APh   Année Philologique

ASP   American Society of Papyrologists

BL   Berichtigungsliste

CIL   Corpus Inscriptionum Latinarum

CMI   Classical Micropublishing Incorporated

COM   Computer-output microfiche

CVA   Corpus Vasorum Antiquorum

IG   Inscriptiones Graecae

LIMC   Lexicon Iconographicum Mythologiae Classicae

MLA   Modern Language Association

PIRS   Philosopher's Information Retrieval System

RIC   Roman Imperial Coinage

SEG   Supplementum Epigraphicum Graecum

TBC   Thesaurus Bibliographiae Classicae

TLG   Thesaurus Linguae Graecae

TLL   Thesaurus Linguae Latinae

UAI   Union Académique Internationale

Part 1

CONCLUSIONS AND RECOMMENDATIONS

Section 1
Introduction

[1.1.1]   The Ad Hoc Committee on Basic Research Tools
undertook three tasks: (1) to discover what work on basic
materials for research in classical studies was already
underway;   (2) to recommend specific tools for which the
need was most pressing in the next decade; and (3)   to
assess the basic directions research tool creation should
take in the future.

[1.1.2]   What we have discovered about work in progress is
reported in Part II of this report.   It is inevitably
incomplete.   We sent a letter of inquiry to the person
supposed to be in charge of the projects which came to our
attention, largely through responses to our principal
questionnaire to the field (see below).   The answers of the
scholars to whom we wrote are the basis of the brief
sketches given, but we are responsible for the form of the
notices below.   We have received a most cordial and
cooperative reception from these colleagues and tender our
thanks to them for their help.

[1.1.3]   We have collected the body of material on which
to base our recommendations by means of a questionnaire
circulated both in North America and abroad.   This
questionnaire and a tabulation of its results are given
in Part III of this report.   To the nearly six hundred
colleagues who shared their thoughts with us we are
grateful.   The decisions taken by the committee on all
points of substance, however, reflect not a mechanical
analysis of the responses to the survey but the considered
judgment of the committee reached in three meetings and in
telephone conversation and written correspondence.   Many
patterns and developments which are only dimly visible
at present to most of the profession came into sharp focus
for the committee as it analyzed and discussed the assembled

material. We have regarded the task of making recommendations for basic directions in work as much more important
than proposing specific projects, but a few such specific
proposals will be found in section [1.8], and we regard
these as having very great importance.

[1.1.4] We wish to express our indebtedness to those who
have made the committee's work possible; above all to the
National Endowment for the Humanities, which granted the
Association the funds to support the committee's activities,
in particular the survey and our meetings, to Columbia
University for providing office and meeting facilities,
and to the staff of the Secretary's office who did much
of the hard clerical work, especially Alberta Fiore Delia,
our graduate research assistant, and Walter Roberts, our
work-study research assistant. Bruce Tetelman and John
Helm of the Columbia University Center for Computing
Activities helped with the processing of the objective
part of the survey results.

Section 2
Basic Principles

[1.2.1]   Before proceeding to our main conclusions, we consider it worthwhile setting out certain principles and values which underlie our report.   These are not merely assumptions, but principles explicitly discussed without which what follows would make little sense.

[1.2.2]   First, classical studies are international both in subject matter and in organization.   This inescapable fact affects all of our judgments.   Very few really important projects are realized by the nationals of a single country, and most individual scholars find their closest ties in research as likely to be across national boundaries as not.   This internationalism is not at all a new development, but it has increased in intensity and complexity since the Second World War with the development of better transportation and communications.   Even with rising travel costs the process is probably irreversible; and in our view it is a good thing, adding perspective to our scholarly work and giving as a side benefit a close acquaintance with other countries and their people which we believe is in the national interest.

[1.2.3]   Secondly, we recognize that classical studies are not a single discipline but a cluster of disciplines interested in understanding the civilizations of the ancient Mediterranean world.   These disciplines - philology, history, philosophy, archaeology, and others - have often divergent needs and at the same time close ties to the same disciplines as the latter deal with other civilizations.   We strongly support the further development of these links.

[1.2.4]   Thirdly, we stress the importance of continuity. The creation of a research project or working tool is costly and difficult, and the history of classical

3

scholarship is littered with projects which were not carried through. A bibliographical reference tool, for example, loses much of its utility if it is not produced consistently and continuously by a staff which changes only gradually.

[1.2.5] Fourthly, we have proceeded on the belief that we must take into account the limitations of available resources in making choices. We live in an era of contracting student population and employment opportunities, in which institutions are ever slower to commit funds, and in which the period of most rapid growth of Federal support for the humanities has probably come to an end, at least for a time, when measured in real dollars. Some of our European colleagues enjoy better circumstances, but many are worse off than we, and there are signs of deterioration there too. We cannot afford everything.

[1.2.6] Fifthly, we support the use of modern technology wherever it is appropriate and believe that those areas where it is appropriate are more numerous than many of our colleagues may consider--although we were pleasantly surprised by the receptiveness of respondents to our questionnaire to several technological developments. At the same time, we insist that computers, microforms and the like are means and not ends, and that their use is appropriate only where an analysis of the needs of a project indicates that the benefits outweigh the headaches.

Section 3
Summary of Recommendations

[1.3.1]   International Projects
1.   That the highest priority be given to the
continuing and stable funding of the major ongoing
international projects in which there is American involvement, whether they have U.S. offices or not;
2.   That some means of more permanent funding for
U.S. offices not directly dependent on periodic applications
be established. As an alternative to the time-consuming
complexities of frequent reapplication, the Committee
suggests that the ACLS is the logical equivalent of the
European academies and that NEH and private foundations
both help provide the funds in a block grant;
3.   That the same channel be used for more ample
support of projects in which American involvement is
passive, as in the case of the Thesaurus Linguae Latinae;
and
4.   That fellowship-granting agencies be willing to
receive applications for junior scholars to spend more
than one year working at the TLL.

[1.3.2]   Thesaurus, Dictionary, Concordance, and Data Bank
1.   That top priority be given to the continued
development of data banks containing classical texts and
bibliographical tools, and to providing direct access to
them by computer terminal through whatever method proves
to be the most effective;
2.   That mechanical compilations, whether by hand or
by machine, be given low priority as involving in most
cases a waste of resources in doing a poor job at what
direct interactive computer use can do;
3.   That a very high priority be given to the creation
of the technical means (e.g. line printers and COM heads)
through which the computer's resources can be used
effectively and economically for classical languages; and

5

4. That support be given to projects for encyclopedic and analytic tools for the study of texts, particularly for the specialized vocabulary of particular branches of literary or documentary texts.

[1.3.3] Accessibility

1. That the APA and NEH view the expansion of the use of data banks through networks as a major contribution to broader access to scholarly material and take the steps needed to bring it to reality; and

2. That NEH provide the revolving capital to allow a rapid growth in the availability of classical scholarship on microfiche.

[1.3.4] Translations and Commentaries

1. That Greek and Latin texts be given a low priority for support for translation within the Research Materials program except where a specific justification is demonstrated;

2. That support be given to translation of crucial works in the less commonly known languages, ancient and modern;

3. That microfiche be the medium of publication for such translations in all cases where materials are expected to have a limited audience; and

4. That financial support for commentaries be directe principally at their publication and not at their creation.

[1.3.5] Some Specific Needs

1. That *APh* be computerized, both for its current bibliography and for the retrospective file, in order to widen the available bibliographical data bank;

2. That other related or specialized bibliographies be entered also, especially *Numismatic Literature, Bibliographie Papyrologique, Bibliographie Linguistique,* the *Byzantinische Zeitschrift* bibliographies, and ultimately the *SEG;*

3. That further textual corpora like *CIL* and the papyri be added to existing machine-readable repositories

as soon as possible;

4. That care be taken to make these and other data banks (like LIMC) mutually compatible;

5. That a major bibliographical effort to bring order into Greek epigraphy be undertaken as a preliminary to the entry of epigraphical texts into the computer;

6. That the need for local prosopographies be met mainly by interactive use of computerized data banks when these are available, but that publication of an up-to-date Athenian prosopography from the card file in Princeton be undertaken; and

7. That the APA sponsor a cartographic project to provide adequate maps and atlases for the study of the classical world.

[1.3.6] We recommend in the light of these needs that the APA establish a standing Committee on Research, smaller than our *ad hoc* committee--we suggest five members-- with staggered fixed terms, to recommend to the Directors appropriate action in all matters relevant to research and to monitor developments in that realm. We recommend further that this committee have such standing or ad hoc subcommittees for individual projects as may be useful, and that persons other than members of the Committee on Research make up part of the membership of these subcommittees. We recommend further that one such subcommittee replace the present TLG Advisory Committee.

Section 4
International Projects

[1.4.1]   American scholars and institutions participate in a variety of scholarly projects carried on by international collaboration.   This participation ranges from the essentially passive, as in the case of the Thesaurus Linguae Latinae (TLL), to which the APA makes a small annual contribution and to the triennial meetings of the council of which it sends one representative, to the very active, as in the case of the Lexicon Iconographicum Mythologiae Classicae (LIMC), for which there is a very active U.S. office involved in the collection of information and all other aspects of the project.   The different situations pose varied problems operationally and financially.

[1.4.2]   The TLL is an example of a project for which the American system provides no adequate basis for support. The APA's contribution represents dues money and cannot be increased significantly without severe problems: substantial dues increases or sharp cutbacks in the APA's own programs.   The most useful support would be an American Ph.D. to work on the TLL for two or three years, acquiring in the process a kind of training unavailable in the U.S., but the cost of such a collaboration would be prohibitive for the APA.   Where European countries send such scholars, the cost is borne by the national academy or by the national research foundation, not by learned associations from dues money.   But it is difficult under existing programs to find support for such a researcher from U.S. sources since the project is not an American one.   In effect, structural differences between the U.S. and European countries seriously hamper U.S. participation in the enterprise.

[1.4.3]   LIMC, on the other hand, exists as an American Office which is the applicant for federal funds.   Here, however, the emphasis is on work carried out in the U.S.

office, not on the work of the central office in Switzerland. Because of the greater decentralization of the LIMC, compared to TLL, this quasi-autonomy is not apparently a serious hindrance. Much the same is true of the *Supplementum Epigraphicum Graecum (SEG)*, the work of which is divided between Berkeley (Attica and the Peloponnesos), and Leiden (everything else). *SEG* has a comparatively minute budget, met in large part by grants from the ACLS and the APA as well as university support. These grants are, like federal ones, for a limited time only. The American Office of *L'Année Philologique*, supported by NEH and the University of North Carolina, is similarly a contributor of material within a limited area which functions not so much by direct involvement in the work of the Paris office as by providing to it a part of the needed material.

[1.4.4] These projects are in general ones where the task involved is large, especially for those aiming not at a single product but at permanence (the continuing bibliographical tools), and international distribution of the burden is beneficial both for the project and for the scholars involved. We believe that a U.S. withdrawal of support for or loss of involvement in such projects would be very damaging to international scholarship and to the reputation of the U.S. in scholarly circles. A retreat into nationally-based projects would be disastrous.

[1.4.5] Funding is a serious problem here. American funding for these projects is largely a matter of triennial grants, which are by no means assured despite the extremely strong support for these projects from the profession documented by our survey and always brought out in NEH reviewers' comments and panels. Preparation of the complex and lengthy application consumes a great deal of time in each cycle, and negotiations with NEH consume even more. Virtually every project director has felt this drain of productive time.

[1.4.6]   Insecurity and wasted time have a common origin in the structure of American funding and in particular the nature of the NEH, dependent itself on triennial reauthorization and annual congressional appropriations.   In Europe such ongoing long-range projects tend to be financed by national or regional academies or other organs with greater permanence than NEH has, although European projects in many cases have their own problems with funding.   The U.S. has no equivalent bodies with any substantial disposable funds The ACLS is our nearest equivalent and our representative to the Union Académique Internationale, but up to now most of its own funds depend on limited grants from NEH and private foundations.   The strengthening of ACLS is a precondition for American effectiveness in collaborating in international projects.

[1.4.7]   The character of grant funding provides another hindrance to American participation in long-range international projects: the ceaseless passion for novelty on the part of granting agencies.   The model dearest to the heart of most granters is the project which can become independent of its support after a short time, allowing the granter to move on to some other 'innovative' project.   Since most granters have established explicit guidelines couched in these terms, the plight of the no-longer-new project is often deplorable.   This model will work in some cases (certain of which are discussed below), but scholarship is only exceptionally analogous to business enterprise.   In our experience, NEH has, despite the problems described in 1.4.6 above, been more receptive than most private foundations to the needs of continuity; but even the Endowment has shown a doctrinaire hostility to continuing support in certain cases, most visibly that of bibliography.

[1.4.8]   A significant part of the cost of those projects with American offices is borne by host institutions (University of North Carolina at Chapel Hill for *APh*,

Rutgers for *LJMC*), usually provided mainly in the form of
salaries for released time and waiver of indirect costs.
These costs are real, but they are usually not obviously
and recognizably additions to the institutions' budgets.
They are thus more palatable than identifiable additional
costs like materials, new staff positions, and travel. The
two projects mentioned have been relatively fortunate in
support, but institutional willingness to contribute to the
cost of other such projects is often inversely proportional
to the institution's reputation. We do not think that most
universities can be expected, over the long run, to pay all
of the costs of these projects, no matter what the gain to
their prestige.

[1.4.9] Some tools may be supportable in the long run by
user fees, whether in the form of publication prices or
through charges for the use of a data bank. With
international projects, however, this approach presents
grave difficulties. With *APh*, for example, the book is
published in France, and it seems unlikely that even if the
price were higher than the present (*ca* $100) the proceeds
would be used to support an American office; it could be
argued that it would be more efficient to add a few
positions in Paris than to keep a separate office.
Additionally, the concept of support from user fees for
research operations is not likely to win support in the
European offices of such projects because of their
tradition of more stable public support.

[1.4.10] <u>Recommendations</u>: In the light of the consider-
ations raised above, the committee recommends the following
measures:

   1. That the highest priority be given to the
continuing and stable funding of the major ongoing international projects in which there is American involvement,
whether they have U.S. offices or not;

   2. That some means of more permanent funding for U.S.
offices, not directly dependent on periodic applications,

be established. As an alternative to the time-consuming complexities of frequent reapplication, the committee suggests that the ACLS is the logical equivalent of the European academies and that NEH and private foundations both help provide the funds in a block grant;

  3.   That the same channel be used for more ample support of projects in which American involvement is passive, as in the case of TLL; and

  4.   That fellowship-granting agencies be willing to receive applications for junior scholars to spend more than one year working at the TLL.

Section 5
Thesaurus, Dictionary, Concordance, and Data Bank

[1.5.1] The core of the areas of classical studies with which we have concerned ourselves is the body of surviving textual material in Greek and Latin, whether preserved by medieval manuscript, inscription on stone, papyrus, ostrakon, or coin. This material has been estimated at some 100,000,000 words, of which 90 per cent is in Greek and 10 per cent in Latin. Scholars need a variety of types of tools to use the texts, and traditionally much of the effort of classical scholarship has gone into producing such tools: dictionaries and lexica, both general and specific; concordances; commentaries; prosopographies; grammars; and so on. These tools fulfill different functions, but they have a common purpose: to allow the scholar to understand the language and content of his text and to find parallel or related texts. We see every reason to believe that classical scholarship will continue to need tools aimed at these needs for the foreseeable future. The results of our survey showed an enormous--but very diffuse--demand for tools of these kinds.

[1.5.2] In the past, all work on such tools was done by hand, and the very conception of these works was rooted in the type of labor used in preparing them. It has been perfectly common for a scholar to spend decades on this type of work. In recent years the coming of automatic data processing has begun to produce a transformation in methods of work. Texts on computer tape have become the basis for preparing concordances particularly, and the ambitious project of the Thesaurus Linguae Graecae promises ultimately to make all of Greek available in machine-readable form. Still more recently, David W. Packard has made considerable progress toward entering the bulk of Latin literature into his Ibycus computer system, and when these tapes are deposited in the APA's Repository of Machine-Readable Texts, an equivalent for the TLG will exist for Latin.

[1.5.3] Although our survey has shown that relatively few
classicists have any present use for these computer
repositories, an enormous number see them as of great
future importance. We concur wholeheartedly; but we
believe that the implications of these developments have
scarcely been perceived even by those involved in these
projects.

[1.5.4] For example, the TLG in its limited efforts to
date to provide services to the profession has set a
relatively high priority on concordances, so far mostly
printed, but increasingly to be on microfiche. Despite the
widespread interest in concordances displayed in our survey
results, we believe that the large-scale production of
concordances is unwise and the printing of such concordances
in book form largely a waste of money. First, the demand
for concordances is diffuse: a handful at most per author
except in the case of a small number of the most popular
authors--precisely those for whom such concordances are
most likely already to exist. These concordances cannot
be produced economically in book form because the market
is too small, even by the standards of the short runs of
specialized scholarship; and even in fiche form, the
initial computer costs of generating these concordances
are large. When they are created they are relatively crude
tools, providing little of the intellectual sophistication
a hand-produced concordance can have and yet hardly using
the computer's true capabilities.

[1.5.5] It is this last failing which to our thinking
condemns the large-scale production of concordances: they
represent the use of modern technology for an antiquated
tool. It is possible already to use a computer to ask
questions about textual material which are far more
sophisticated and interesting than those a concordance can
answer. Such interactive use of the computer, in which a
question can be progressively refined by the user, is a

routine matter in many fields of computer applications.
The Ibycus system now has extremely powerful searching
programs to make such interrogation even of very large
quantities of material possible. It is our conviction
that direct access to data banks of classical texts through
computer terminals will prove a far more sophisticated,
useful, and economical tool than a vast array of printed
or filmed concordances or similar works.

[1.5.6] In short, traditional tools for the study of texts
will retain their utility only to the extent that they
transcend mechanical assemblage of examples, an activity
done much more efficiently and accurately by machine. Many
works will simply become obsolete; others (dictionaries,
especially) will still be useful insofar as their analysis
of meanings and usage is worthwhile, but the user will look
elsewhere for citations. For this reason we believe that
priority in dictionary projects should in the future go to
encyclopedic dictionaries which analyze the usage and
substance of words and provide references to other
discussions, not to compilations of citations. Berger's
Encyclopedic Dictionary of Roman Law and the great Kittel
Theological Dictionary of the New Testament are examples.
To other types of lexica or dictionaries we would give a
low priority.

[1.5.7] It is far from clear what form access to computerized data banks will take. The present is a time of
extremely rapid development, and no system devised now will
be quite permanent. For example, among the questions to be
considered are: (1) Will a single national data bank or
several regional ones be preferable? (2) Will such a data
bank be independent or part of a major network? (3) If it
is part of a network, will this be one of the major commercial contractors (for example, MLA's bibliography is
available from Lockheed) or a non-profit university-based
network? There are other questions too, and addressing
them is a major task for the next few years.

[1.5.8] A major concomitant of the developments we have
outlined must be the creation of the technology to make them
usable for classics. Packard's Ibycus system can display
Greek on a computer terminal; but there is no analogous
high-quality line printer which can print Greek (nothing
between very poor printers and high-quality but very
expensive photocomposition equipment), nor any apparatus
for creating computer-output microfiche (COM) directly
without going through a paper copy. These are necessary
for the proper and economical use of classical material on
computer, and we urge the NEH to assume leadership in
supporting their development. The APA's publisher,
Scholars Press, has already taken steps toward the creation
of a COM apparatus.

[1.5.9]   Recommendations:
     1. That top priority be given to the continued
development of data banks containing classical texts and
bibliographical tools, and to providing direct access to
them by computer terminal through whatever method proves
to be the most effective.
     2. That mechanical compilations, whether by hand or
by machine, be given low priority as involving in most
cases a waste of resources in doing a poor job at what
direct interactive computer use can do;
     3. That a very high priority be given to the creation
of the technical means, (e.g. line printers and COM heads),
through which the computer's resources can be used effectively and economically for classical languages; and
     4. That support be given to projects for encyclopedic
and analytic tools for the study of texts, particularly for
the specialized vocabulary of literary or documentary
texts.

Section 6
Accessibility

[1.6.1] There is enormous inequality in the U.S. in the degree to which scholars have access to research materials. In some senses these inequalities diminished during the last two decades by virtue of the generous budgets once enjoyed by many newer state institutions and of the wide availability of copying machines. But the days of lavish budgets are over, and no one is so optimistic as to believe they will return. And there remains a great gulf between the resources available to those at the top 15 or 20 institutions and what the rest have to put up with.

[1.6.2] In the 1960's the gaps might have seemed tolerable because temporary: they were narrowing; and in any case demand for faculty was so strong that almost anyone interested in research could hope ultimately for a position which would allow him to have major facilities. This is no longer true. Most major institutions have stable if not declining faculties, heavily staffed with professors in their 40's to early 50's. Jobs are scarce, and numerous young scholars of promise have found themselves in colleges or universities with poor research facilities, burdened by the knowledge that a better position would come only from exceptional scholarly productivity, but that their present institution offered few means of doing the necessary research. There is still some upward mobility for the very able and determined, but many competent people will be in institutions without research resources for years to come. Many of them want to continue scholarly activity but find that circumstances discourage it.

[1.6.3] There is little the APA can do to help the basic demographic and economic trends involved in these developments, and NEH itself is in no position--despite energetic and valuable attempts to deal with certain

17

aspects of the problem--to provide more than palliatives. Fellowships and summer research support, for example, can help, especially for those with heavy teaching loads. But we affirm that research is an activity which must be carried on fairly consistently to have hope of being current and of good quality. The only reasonable hope of improving the working lives of these members of our profession is to make available to them where they live and work the main research materials necessary for their scholarly endeavors.

[1.6.4] The increased tightness of institutional budgets, battered by energy costs and salary raises (inadequate though they may be), on the one hand, and the rapidly rising costs of books and especially journals, on the other, has made this ideal of local ability to meet needs for research even more elusive. Even major universities, for that matter, cannot afford the coverage they once could. The recent report of the 'National Enquiry into Scholarly Communication' (Scholarly Publishing, John Hopkins Press, 1979) makes various proposals aimed at alleviating present problems for scholars in general. These lie beyond the scope of our report, but within the classics. We suggest two major means of improving the situation:

[1.6.5] (1) The availability of the bulk of ancient texts--and, in time, major bibliographic tools--via a networked computer data bank, such as we advocate in section 1.5 above, will bring a huge mass of material into easy reach by computer terminal. Terminals will be universally available in the coming decade at very reasonable cost (especially compared to the price of books), and while telecommunication costs are not likely to be negligible, they are likely to rise more slowly than salaries, printing, and travel, to name three major components of traditional research expenses. The democratizing potential of the databank and terminal should not be underestimated. At the same time, there will be a great

need for classicists to be given basic training in the
proper use of computers and the data banks to which they
give access. For a limited time, special summer institutes
may well be needed to train scholars who are already active
but to whom computerized resources have become newly
available.

[1.6.6] (2) It will take some time for this system to be
fully effective; and it is not in any case clear as yet to
what extent material other than the texts themselves will
be electronically available in the foreseeable future.
There will still be no substitute for a well-stocked
library. This library's holdings, however, need not be
entirely in book form. Printed or typed material can be
reproduced on microfiche and sold, profitably, at a savings
of 75-90% over the price of the same material in printed
and bound paper form. There is some skepticism about the
willingness of classicists to use microfiche, but this
doubt is not well-founded. Our survey showed that 88% of
the respondents were willing to use microfiche in view of
the economic factors described.

[1.6.7] Not a great deal is available currently on microfiche in classical studies. The American Society of
Papyrologists has published two series of 'Papyrology on
Microfiche' which have sold well and been widely accepted
in that discipline. A certain amount is available from
commercial venders, notably a Swiss firm IDC, but commercial
prices are generally about triple those of the ASP.and thus
not nearly so attractive to those interested in lower costs.
The APA and ASP have jointly begun a major program under
the name of Classical Micropublishing Incorporated, which
has made several major reference works available. But an
almost total lack of capital has caused this program to
begin very slowly. We suggest that the NEH consider a
significant grant to CMI to serve as revolving capital and
to allow the APA to expand availability of microforms in
classical studies.

[1.6.8]   <u>Recommendations</u>:

    1.   That the APA and NEH view the expansion of the use
of data banks through networks as a major contribution to
broader access to scholarly material and take the steps
needed to bring it to reality; and

    2.   That NEH provide the revolving capital to allow
a rapid growth in the availability of classical scholarship
on microfiche.

Section 7
Translations and Commentaries

[1.7.1] The committee was asked by the Endowment to include translations and commentaries in its deliberations and survey, because these fall under the Research Materials programs of the Research Division. The original mandate from the Directors was defined as 'Basic Research Tools.' We remain skeptical that various categories of translations have much in common with the other problems dealt with here or with each other.

[1.7.2] We distinguish within translations two basic categories: those of primary evidence--ancient authors and documents--and those of secondary works. Within each of these, we distinguish further between works written originally in languages normally essential to classical scholars and those written in other languages. Each of these evokes different responses.

[1.7.3] Under normal circumstances, translations of most Greek and Latin authors of antiquity are not research tools. This does not, of course, mean that they are not useful; they are, indeed, a characteristic and valuable end-product of the study of the classics and deserve support, where needed, as such. There are, however, instances where the bulk or technical difficulty of a textual corpus makes a translation a major tool of scholarly interpretation: We think especially of Justinian's *Digest*, a translation of which, under the direction of Alan Watson, has just been committed to press (Harvard University Press) or of some of the bulkier Greek authors, especially of the Roman period. But in general, any classical research worthy of the name must be based on the Greek and Latin texts, not translations.

[1.7.4] From the classicist's point of view, ancient sources in nonclassical (i.e., not Hellenic or Italic) languages such as Akkadian, Egyptian, Persian, Arabic and the like present a different question. Few classicists will learn these languages, and yet some material in them is of undeniable importance to the study of classical antiquity. Translations of these texts--preferably accompanied by good commentaries--deserve support. We are aware, of course, that the Semiticist or Egyptologist may have exactly the same view about classical texts; but they are more likely to know classical languages than we e.g. Egyptian, and we do not conclude that translations of classical texts even so become important research tools to classicists. In any event, Greek and Latin are far better served than other ancient literatures in respect to translations.

[1.7.5] As in the case of Greek and Latin authors, so with modern works in major foreign languages (which are for most purposes French, German and Italian). No scholar can conduct research in any area of classics without a decent reading knowledge of these languages, and the amount published in them is so large that an effort to translate enough that the German-less classicist could do research would be futile. The solution is certainly, as the recent report of the Presidential Commission on Foreign Language and International Studies emphasized, better language training for Americans. It remains true that some really fundamental works of synthesis have classroom application and deserve translation for that reason; but we do not see this as having anything to do with research tools.

[1.7.6] Not all secondary scholarship is written in the major international languages. Individual scholars may find that their specialty requires them to learn the modern language of an area which interests them or in which a lot on a particular subject has been published. And it is hard to have much sympathy for the scholar who claims to know German but balks at the occasional Dutch article or even book. Still, enough is published in Slavic languages, especially Russian, in Turkish, in Arabic, and in Hebrew, that no one can hope to read every language which may turn up in the course of his work. It is questionable, however, that more than a tiny fraction of such material has an interest for a large enough group of scholars as to warrant the expenditure of substantial sums of public funds to translate and publish it. (It often appears that material published in such languages either is republished in a major language or is not of sufficient importance to warrant translation.) We urge great care in this area and the use of microfiche to keep costs within reasonable limits.

[1.7.7] We emphasize again that translations have many uses, and that the skepticism we have expressed has to do only with their role as research tools. It is worth pointing out that translations as research materials were given uniformly low priorities by the respondents to our survey, even by those who teach courses in translation and by those who do not teach in major research institutions. In only a handful of fields (Philosophy, Religion, Science, History of Ideas, Renaissance Literature, Education) did even translations of primary works get as high a vote as random distribution of votes would have yielded. Our view is not in any sense a rejection of the importance of translations in college education.

[1.7.8] Commentaries offer different problems. There are numerous ones for some popular works of great literature, but none or only extremely outdated ones for many authors of lesser literary interest but nonetheless great importance for the study of antiquity. Few of these authors attract first-rate commentators, for understandable reasons: scholars with literary interest are not moved to spend many years commenting on an author of little intrinsic literary worth, and few historians choose commentaries as their preferred form of publication. We affirm the need for more such commentaries to authors other than the obvious ones already well-covered.

[1.7.9] We are not so sure that commentaries need
significant financial support at the stage of creation,
however. Fellowship support for free time is certainly
appropriate, but the elaborate and costly framework of major
research projects is rarely appropriate. We do, however,
think the Endowment should give commentaries a high priority
in the allocation of funds for publication costs, which are
unavoidably high for such complicated works. We stress also
that access to an author's text via computer terminal is
virtually necessary in the case of most authors and may
improve the quality of commentaries greatly, especially in
the case of voluminous authors.

[1.7.10]   Recommendations:

1. That Greek and Latin texts be given a low priority
for support for translation within the Research Materials
program except where a specific justification is
demonstrated;

2. That support be given to translation of crucial
works in the less commonly known languages, ancient and
modern;

3. That microfiche be the medium of publication for
such translations in all cases where materials are expected
to have a limited audience; and

4. That financial support for commentaries be directed
principally at their publication and not at their creation.

Section 8
Some Specific Needs

[1.8.1] It would be pointless for the committee to offer
here its views in great detail on how the major ongoing
projects should be managed, and we do not presume to do so.
We do, however, have certain general remarks about
directions to be taken. Some of these have already been
mentioned: the need to conceive of both the lexicographic
projects (TLG, APA Repository of Machine Readable Texts)
and the bibliographic or descriptive ones (*APh, LIMC, SEG*),
in terms not only of publications but above all of data
banks available for direct consultation is to our mind the
single most pressing necessity. LIMC has shown impressive
leadership in this regard, and the MLA provides a somewhat
different model for a bibliographic tool. We suggest that
the movement of *APh* to a system analogous to or even
essentially identical to that of MLA (with the addition of
the abstracts) is extremely important, and that the computerization of the back file of the *APh* is also highly
desirable. We urge also that expert technical advice be
employed to ensure that these various systems develop
compatibly and in a manner to encourage rather than
discourage the average, not very technically-minded,
classicist user.

[1.8.2] These data banks will not in themselves be
sufficient, however. A massive effort is needed to add
other existing bodies of material to memory and similarly
to make them accessible. The *Numismatic Literature*
published by the American Numismatic Society; the
Bibliographie Papyrologique on cards published by the
Fondation Egyptologique Reine Elisabeth in Brussels; parts
of the *Bibliographie Linguistique*; and the bibliography
published in each issue of *Byzantinische Zeitschrift* all
would widen, deepen, and generally improve the resource
constituted by *Aph* and we urge their inclusion in data banks

25

at an early date.

[1.8.3] Similarly, there are huge masses of textual
material still to be captured in machine-readable form.
Some of these are literary works for which it is difficult
or impossible to find a usable edition. This more than
anything has slowed data-entry at the TLG. Others are
documents, which pose great problems of format and coding
to the computer. TLG has had to renounce, for lack of the
matching funds, an NEH grant for developing a codebook for
the papyri, which are the best-organized group of documents.
The solution of these problems is a very high priority in
our opinion. On the Latin side, too, the recording on tape
of CIL and other epigraphical publications would help a
great deal, and we urge its importance.

[1.8.4] In Greek epigraphy, however, the situation is still
worse. The dispersal of texts is enormous: IG covers only
part of the Greek world, while others have regional or local
corpora or none at all; *SEG* (in its previous existence)
gave only the spottiest of coverage. A major bibliographical labor, the creation of a checklist of publications of
inscriptions, is the indispensable preliminary to the entry
of texts. Such a bibliography would itself need to be
automated and must contain corrections and discussions
of texts as well as editions. It is in our view a project
of the first importance.

[1.8.5] A considerable number of survey respondents cited
the need for regional or local prosopographies of all parts
of the Greek world as a major desideratum. In general, we
agree wholeheartedly. For most areas, the computerization
of the texts (and before that, the bibliographic canon
discussed above), seem to us indispensable preliminaries.
Interest in most individual Greek cities is relatively
limited, and either a microfiche prosopography or perhaps
simply the ability to search the data bank would be
sufficient. In the case of Athens, however, the importance
and interest of the city warrant a book-form publication;

and the material for it exists already in card-file form at the Institute for Advanced Study in Princeton. We recommend its publication as of the highest interest to classical studies.

[1.8.6] We come, finally, to an area of extremely great importance, where the state of our tools is utterly disastrous, cartography. There is hardly anything more important to understanding ancient history than a clear conception of the terrain on which its events took place. But the best available maps, the old Kiepert ones, are virtually unavailable, and nothing really useful has become available for most areas in the last few decades. The *Tabula Imperii Romani* proceeds at a snail's pace, parcelled out among the modern countries its sheets cover (not always those where the best scholars for the purpose are found), and appearing, when it does, in different styles everywhere. A concerted attempt to produce a uniform series of maps which show both the topography--with all the sophistication of modern cartography--and the ancient toponyms--with the accumulated knowledge of classical scholarship--would be immensely valuable.

[1.8.7]   Recommendations:

1. That *APh* be computerized both for its current bibliography and for the retrospective file in order to widen the available bibliographical data bank;

2. That other related or specialized bibliographies be entered also, especially *Numismatic Literature*, *Bibliographie Papyrologique*, *Bibliographie Linguistique*, the *Byzantinische Zeitschrift* bibliographies, and ultimately the *SEG*;

3. That further textual corpora like *CIL* and the papyri be added to existing machine readable repositories as soon as possible;

4. That care be taken to make these and other data banks (like LIMC) mutually compatible;

5. That a major bibliographical effort to bring order

into Greek epigraphy be undertaken as a preliminary to the entry of epigraphical texts into the computer;

6.   That the need for local prosopographies be met mainly by interactive use of·computerized data banks when these are available, but that publication of an up-to-date Athenian prosopography from the card file in Princeton be undertaken; and

7.   That the APA sponsor a cartographic project to provide adequate maps and atlases for the study of the classical world.

Section 9
Organization

[1.9.1] One of the most striking results of our survey was the abundance of information it produced on projects of which the 13 members of the committee knew little or nothing, despite their diverse specialties. We were also impressed by the diversity of forms taken by projects and of types of sponsorship. These conditions, however, carry a significant risk of fostering unproductive duplication of work and the failure to undertake certain necessary projects altogether.

[1.9.2] We believe it would be in the interest of the APA to have a means of monitoring more continuously developments in the area of research tools, of supervising the Association's involvement with those to which it has a direct connection, and of encouraging the undertaking of projects it considers needed. For example, the APA has a committee at present to advise TLG, but this committee satisfies neither the TLG nor the committee itself with its lack of any direct connection to APA policy decisions or positions concerning the TLG.

[1.9.3] We recommend, therefore, that the APA establish a standing Committee on Research, smaller than our *ad hoc* committee--we suggest five members with staggered fixed terms, to recommend to the Directors appropriate action in all matters relevant to research and to monitor developments in that realm. We recommend further that this committee have such standing or ad hoc subcommittees for individual projects as may be useful, and that persons other than members of the Committee on Research make up part of the membership of these subcommittees. We recommend further that one such subcommittee replace the present TLG Advisory Committee.

Part 2

WORK IN PROGRESS

The information presented below is summarized--
accurately, we hope--by us from material provided to us by
the persons named in each case. For one reason or another
we failed to get information about many projects, and these
do not appear here. Nor do those already completed and
published (with a few exceptions which we judged useful),
those in very embryonic form, and those abandoned. We hope
that what remains will nonetheless be of use and interest.

BIBLIOGRAPHIC WORKS

Année Philologique

Central Office: In charge: Juliette Ernst.   11, avenue
    René-Coty, 75014 Paris, France
American Office: In charge: William C. West III,
    212 Murphey Hall 030A, University of North Carolina,
    Chapel Hill, NC 27514.

The volumes of *APh* continue to appear regularly about 20
months after the end of the year which they concern; vol.49
(1978) is the most recent.   The work of preparing slips is
divided among offices in Chapel Hill, Heidelberg, and Paris
(where the bulk of the work is done), with collaboration
in several other countries.   The work involved and the size
of the volume continue to grow with the output of books and
articles.   Neither the cost of the volume nor its interval
from the year covered seems likely to diminish with present
methods.   Remarks about the Committee's recommendations for
APh can be found in Part 1.

Thesaurus Bibliographiae Classicae

Director: Rodrigue La Rue, Dept. of Classics, Université
    du Québec à Trois-Rivières, Case Postale 500, Trois
    Rivières, P.Q., G9A 5H7, Canada.

The TBC aims at collecting and computerizing the complete
retrospective bibliography of classical studies, including
L'Année Philologique and other compilations.   Work so far has
been devoted to the collection of bibliographical dossiers
and creating the list of periodicals with their
abbreviations.   More work on these stages is needed before
the project can proceed to the computerization of its files.

Dictionary of Bibliographic Abbreviations Used in Classical Scholarship

Jean Susorney Wellington, Classics Library, University of
   Cincinnati, Cincinnati, OH 45221.

The dictionary aims to collect all abbreviations of
periodicals, series, and standard works used in classical
scholarship. It is planned to include an alphabetical list
of abbreviations and full bibliographic descriptions. Most
of the work has been completed except for a possible list
of Congresses and Conferences.

GREEK LANGUAGE AND LITERATURE

Thesaurus Linguae Graecae

Director: Theodore F. Brunner, Thesaurus Linguae Graecae,
    University of California, Irvine, CA 92717.

The TLG is intended to be a complete computerized data bank
of Greek literature and documents written before AD 700,
estimated to total 90,000,000 words. All efforts to date
have been spent on entering the texts, and some 52,000,000
words have been entered so far, of which about half have
been checked and are in principle ready to be converted to
tapes suitable for use. A much lower priority has been
given to creating products from the data banks, but some
10 concordances and indexes have been published so far. At
present the TLG is in the midst of a reassessment to
determine the most fruitful direction of work in the next
few years.

Lexicon der Frühgriechischen Epos

Eva-Maria Voigt, Editor, Seminar für Klassische Philologie,
    Universität Hamburg, Von-Melle-Park 6, 2000 Hamburg 13,
    Germany (BRD)

The remainder of the lexicon is envisaged to take 10
installments of 144 pages each, of which the first (B- about
δόρπον) is expected to be ready for press at the end of
1980.

Index Verborum to Aristotle, *POETICS*

John Crossett, Dept. of Classical and Modern Languages,
    Cornell College, Mount Vernon, IA 52314

The Index has been complete but unpublished for a decade.
Its creator has used it in preparing a translation and

commentary of the *Poetics*, but there are no definite plans
for publication.

A Bibliography of the Galenic Corpus

K.R. Walters (Dept. of Greek and Latin, Wayne State
   University, Detroit, MI 48202) and R.F.Kotrc.

Published in *Transactions and Studies of the College of Physicians
of Philadelphia* n.s.5.1 (1979) 256-304, this bibliography
lists the edition of each Galenic text chosen for entry by
the TLG and various information about each; it is an
outgrowth of the TLG's medical writers project funded by
NEH.   References to the location in the TLG data bank of
each entered item are included.

Lexicon to Diodorus Siculus

Iain McDougall, Dept. of Classics, University of Winnipeg,
   Winnipeg R3B 2E9, Canada

The completed manuscript is being typed and a means of
publication sought.

Concordance: Diodorus Siculus

Catherine Rubincam, Dept. of Classics, Erindale Campus,
   University of Toronto, Mississauga, Ont. L5L 7C6, Canada

The first version of the concordance has been produced; a
second, revised version is to be made available on
microfiche, probably late in 1980.   The TLG tape was used
as base.

Gregory of Nazianzus: Critical Edition

Director: Martin Sicherl, Institut für Altertumskunde,
   Westfälische Wilhelms-Universität, Domplatz 20-22,
   4400 Münster, Germany

The project aims to produce a complete critical edition of
Gregory's works, including those preserved only in
translations into Oriental languages. Professor Sicherl is
preparing the poetry, while a team in Louvain is doing the
Greek speeches (J. Mossay) and oriental versions (G. Garitte).
Extensive preparatory work is currently in progress. A
Symposium Nazianzenum will be held at Louvain in August, 1981.

Commentary to Herodotus

W.G. Forrest, New College, Oxford, OX1 3BN, England

Volume II (5.23-end) is planned to appear first; preparation
is well advanced but writing remains. Volume 1 is in an
earlier stage of preparation.

Concordance: Hippocratic Corpus

Gilles Maloney and Winnie Frohn, Dépt. des Littératures,
   Université Laval, Québec, P.Q. G1K 7P4, Canada

This recently-completed project ('Projet Hippo') has
produced, by computer, a lemmatized concordance to the
Hippocratic corpus. The team is proceeding beyond this to
further studies on the plants in the corpus and on
stylometric analysis.

Index Verborum to Longinus

John Crossett, Dept. of Classical and Modern Languages,
   Cornell College, Mount Vernon, IA 52314

This Index, done first for key words only, is in
preparation in a complete version.

Index Verborum Plutarcheus

Edward N. O'Neil, Dept. of Classics, University of Southern
    California, University Park, Los Angeles, CA 90007

The Index is in next to final form in a MS of 9,000 pages;
a final check is still needed. It was begun in 1940 by
William Helmbold. The method is entirely manual; no
definite publication plans have yet been made.

Prosopography to Old Comedy

Ian C. Storey, Dept. of Classical Studies, Trent University,
    Peterborough, Ont. K9J 7B8, Canada

Part of this work was presented as a B.Phil. thesis at
Oxford, and the rest is in preparation, with the target
date for completion of the MS 1981 or 1982.

Corpus Medicorum Graecorum

Jutta Harig-Kollesch, Akademie der Wissenschaften der DDR,
    Zentralinstitut für Alte Greschichte Leipzigerstr., 3/4
    108 Berlin (DDR)

The long process of preparing critical editions of medical
writers continues, with some 20 assignments currently
outstanding.

Lessico dei Romanzi Greci

Fabrizio Conca, Edoardo De Carli, Giuseppe Zanetto:
    Istituto di Filologia Classica, Università degli Studi,
    Via Festa del Perdono 7, 20122 Milano, Italy

The material is all slipped and lemmatized, and a first
volume (A-Δ) is to appear in 1981 at Edizioni Ateneo e
Bizzarri, Rome. Meanings and uses are given.

LATIN LANGUAGE AND LITERATURE

Thesaurus Linguae Latinae

Director: P. Flury, Thesaurus Linguae Latinae,
   Marstallplat 8, 8000 München 22, Germany (BRD)

The first volume of *TLL* appeared in 1900, and it has now reached the letter P (advancing on two fronts). Work is carried on in Munich by a fulltime staff plus fellows sent by several of the participating countries. It is estimated that at present rates another four decades will be needed for the completion of the *TLL*.

Concordance: Ammianus Marcellinus

G.J.D. Archbold, Dept. of Classics, University of Victoria,
   P.O.Box 1700, Victoria, BC V8W 2Y2, Canada

Published by the University of Toronto Press on microfiche, computer-generated, and based on the Seyfarth edition.

Asconius: Historical Commentary

B.A. Marshall, Dept. of Classics, University of New England,
   Armidale, NSW 2351, Australia

This commentary is now complete in MS; its publication by Arno Press is anticipated.

Concordance: Cato and Varro

W.W. Briggs, Jr., Dept. of Foreign Languages, University of South Carolina, Columbia, SC 29208.

This concordance, prepared from a tape of the APA Repository is ready for composition, which will be carried out by an Ibycus system.

Concordance: Claudian

P.G. Christiansen, Dept. of Classical Languages, Texas Tech
    University, Box 4649, Lubbock, TX 79409

The basic plans have been completed, but actual work is
awaiting funding.

ANCIENT HISTORY

Dictionary of Ancient Geography

Giovanni Forni, Via Cino da Pistoia 3, 00152 Roma, Italy

Ca 70,000 citations collected so far.

Lexicon of Greek Personal Names

Chairman: P.M. Fraser, All Souls College, Oxford OX1, 4AL,
   England

The collection of material is about 3/4 complete, the
processing and editing of computerized slips some way
behind. A major volume covering Greece, the Balkans, Magna
Graecia, Sicily, Western Asia Minor, the Aegean, and South
Russia is planned to be ready for the press by the end of
1984.

Handbook of the Roman Imperial Army

Michael P. Speidel, Dept. of History, University of Hawaii,
   2550 Campus Road, Honolulu, HI 96822

This volume is planned as a part of the *Handbuch der
Altertumswissenschaft* series published by C.H. Beck; the
work of collecting material is well advanced, but the
writing is still in an early stage. The author hopes to
complete his work in 1982.

PHILOSOPHY

Philosopher's Information Retrieval System

Philosophy Documentation Center, Bowling Green State
University, Bowling Green, OH 43403

The data base of PIRS is the bibliographical material
published in *The Philosopher's Index*, supplemented from
a variety of sources including a Retrospective Indexing
Project. It can be consulted on-line through Lockheed
Dialog Retrieval System.

ROMAN LAW

Justinian's *Digest,* Translation

Alan Watson, Law School, University of Pennsylvania, 3400
Chestnut Street I4, Philadelphia, PA 19104

The manuscript has been delivered to Harvard University
Press for publication.

GREEK AND LATIN EPIGRAPHY

IG I^3

D.M. Lewis, Christ Church, Oxford, OX1 1DP, England

Fascicle 1 (Nos. 1-500) is in page proof and expected in 1981; Fascicle 2 (Nos. 501-1500) is complete in manuscript but undergoing revision for a target publication date of 1987.

Grammar of Attic Inscriptions

Leslie Threatte, Dept. of Classics, Dwinelle Hall,
   University of California, Berkeley, CA 94720

Volume 1 (Phonology) appeared in 1980. Volume 2 (Morphology) is still in the early stages of preparation.

Inschriften Griechischer Städte aus Kleinasien

Director: Reinhold Merkelbach, Institut für Altertumskunde
   Universität zu Köln, Albertus-Magnus-Platz, 5000 Köln 41
   Germany

This series includes mostly corpora of individual cities of Asia Minor, produced as circumstances and resources allow without a fixed program. Twenty volumes have been published or announced, taking up some 12 cities (including Ephesos). A prospectus is available from Rudolf Habelt Verlag, Bonn.

Inscriptions Grecques et Latines de la Syrie

Institut Fernand-Courby, Université de Lyon II, Maison de
   l'Orient, 1 rue Raulin, 69007 Lyon, France. (Information
   from Jean-Paul Rey-Coquais)

Seven volumes appeared between 1929 and 1970; VIII,3 has just appeared, and VIII,1 and 2 (Beirut and environs) and XIII (Bostra) are in preparation. Volumes IX–XII are still in the planning stage.

Inscriptions grecques et latines de Jordanie

Institut Fernand-Courby, Université de Lyon II, Maison de
    l'Orient, 1 rue Raulin, 69007 Lyon, France.
    (Information from Jean-Paul Rey-Coquais)

This new series will shortly be inaugurated with volumes on the central and southern regions by P.L. Gatier and M. Sartre; another on Gerasa is in preparation.

Data Bank of Latin Inscriptions

E.J. Jory, University of Western Australia, Nedlands,
    Australia.

CIL VI was placed in the computer in the 1960's and used to produce the indices to *CIL* VI published in 1974–75. A discussion of the project appears in *BICS* 20 (1973) 146–47; *Antiquités Africanes* 9 (1975) 15–22.

Inscriptions Romaines de la Péninsule Ibérique

Robert Etienne, Centre Pierre Paris (ERA 522), Université
    de Bordeaux III, 33405 Talence, France.

A fascicle for the province of Lugo was published in 1979, and several other provinces are in preparation in Bordeaux, Barcelona, and elsewhere.

Bibliographie des Carmina Latina Epigraphica

G. Sanders, Seminarie voor Postklassiek en Middeleeuws
    Latijn, Rijksuniversiteit Gent, Blandijnberg 2, 9000
    Gent, Belgium.

This bibliography of over 3,5000 items has been completed
and will shortly be in press.

PAPYROLOGY

Corpora Papyrorum Graecarum

Directors: Orsolina Montevecchi, Istituto de Papirologia, Università Cattolica del Sacro Cuore, Largo Gemelli 1, 20123 Milano, Italy; Dario Del Corno, Istituto di Papirologia, Università degli Studi, Via Festa del Perdono 3, 20122 Milano, Italy

The Corpora are a series of collections of papyri according to types of document. Individual volumes will, for example, collect epikrisis documents, apprenticeship contracts, death notices, orders for arrest, etc. Some 25 volumes are planned so far, of which four are ready for press.

Berichtigungsliste der Griechischen Papyrusurkunden aus Ägypten

In Charge: P.W. Pestman, Papyrologisch Instituut, Rijksuniversiteit Leiden, Breestraat 155A, 2311 CN Leiden, Netherlands.

The material for volume 7 is now almost completed; it will contain a list of papyri of which photographs have been published in publications other than the original edition of the papyri. Volume 8 has been begun; it is hoped that it will be a comprehensive volume which will replace volumes 1-5. In the meantime, the *TLG* has published a microfiche index to vols. 1-6 of the *BL*.

Grammar of The Greek Papyri of the Roman and Byzantine Periods

Francis T. Gignac, S.J., Dept. of Biblical Studies, Caldwell Hall, Catholic University of America, Washington, DC 20064

49

Volume I (Phonology) appeared in 1976 (Milano, Cisalpino-La Goliardica). Volume II (Morphology) is due to be published in late 1980. Volume III (Syntax) is still in the early stages of preparation and is not expected to be published sooner than 1985 at the earliest.

Grundzüge und Chrestomathie der Papyruskunde I, new edition

Information from Alan K. Bowman, Christ Church, Oxford OX1 1DP, England

A team made up of A.K. Bowman, P.J. Parsons, J.C. Shelton, and J.D. Thomas has undertaken to produce a new edition of Wilcken's classic introduction to papyri. The authors have chosen a format and outline for the work; at present the selection of texts for the *Chrestomathie* is in progress.

Catalogue of Greek and Latin Literary Papyri from Egypt

Paul Mertens, Seminaire de Papyrologie, Université de Liège Liège, Belgium

The second edition of this work by R.A. Pack (Ann Arbor 1965) is in need of complete revision, which is being undertaken by a team headed by Professor Mertens and in contact with Professor Pack. The project is still in the stage of assembling the bibliography, and no completion date is yet projected.

Corpus Papyrorum Christianorum

E.A. Judge, School of History, Macquarie University, North Ryde, NSW, Australia 2113

The project aims to collect and study systematically the papyrus evidence for the history of Christianity. A corpus republishing the documentary texts is in preparation, as well as secondary studies produced along the way.

Corpus of Grammatical Papyri

Alfons Wouters, Departement Klassieke Studies, Katholieke
Universiteit Leuven, Blijde Inkomststraat 21, 3000
Leuven, Belgium

A. Wouters has undertaken an annotated corpus of all the Greek and Latin grammatical tractates preserved on papyri or parchments from Egypt. A first volume: *The Grammatical Papyri from Graeco-Roman Egypt. Contributions to the Study of the 'Ars Grammatica' in Antiquity,* provides an edition with commentary of 16 grammatical manuals and of 9 scholarly treatises. A second volume containing the two remaining categories of grammatical texts on papyri, viz. the exercises and commentaries, will be published in the near future.

ANTIQUITY AND CHRISTIANITY

Reallexikon für Antike und Christentum

Franz-Joseph Dölger-Institut, Universität Bonn

Volume 10 has now been completed and 3 fascicles of volume 11 issued (Girlande - Gnosis).

The Vocabulary of the Greek Testament

E.A. Judge, School of History, Macquarie University, North Ryde, NSW, Australia 2113

A team at Macquarie proposes to revise Moulton and Milligan, *Vocabulary of the Greek Testament*, in the light of the much larger quantity of documentary sources for Koine Greek available now than in 1919-1929, as well as the greater sophistication in our understanding of documentary Greek. The project is currently in the planning stage.

Guide to the Basic Reference Sources for the Study of Eastern Christianity

Sidney Griffith and Janet Timbie, Dept. of Semitic Languages, Catholic University of America, Washington, DC 20064

This annotated bibliography will include listings of reference works pertinent to all branches of Eastern Christianity.

NUMISMATICS

Historia Nummorum, 3rd edition

C.M. Kraay, Heberden Coin Room, Ashmolean Museum, Oxford
OX1 2PH, England

This project, begun by E.S.G. Robinson, aims to replace the
second edition with a series of fascicles, of which that
on Italy will be the first; it is hoped to send it to the
printer by the middle of 1981. The new edition will
exclude Greek Imperial issues, will include every issue
and variety within its defined scope, will illustrate all
principal types, and will provide more ample commentary.

Sylloge Nummorum Graecorum: American Numismatic Society

In charge: Nancy Waggoner, American Numismatic Society,
Broadway at 155th St., New York, NY 10032

Four fascicles have appeared to date; one on Palestine and
Arabia is ready for printing, and another (the remainder
of Sicily) is in preparation. Fifty fascicles in all are
expected, with one to be published every two years.

The Society also publishes a series of *Ancient Coins in
North American Collections,* of which one volume has
appeared and another is in press; it aims at publishing
small but significant collections.

Roman Imperial Coinage V,1

Cathy E. King, Heberden Coin Room, Ashmolean Museum, Oxford,
OX1 2PH, England

Part of *RIC* V is currently being revised; it covers the
years 253-270. Work is currently in the early stages of
collecting material and will not be copmpleted sooner than
in five years.

MEDIEVAL AND RENAISSANCE LATIN AND GREEK

Catalogus Translationum et Commentariorum

Secretary of Executive Committee: F. Edward Cranz,
    Connecticut College, New London, CT 06320

The *Catalogus* provides bibliographies of all traceable Latin
translations of and commentaries on ancient Greek and Latin
authors written in the Middle Ages and Renaissance.
Four volumes have been published to date (1960, 1971, 1974,
1980), and the material for V is largely in hand, with
numerous assignments outstanding. Grants from NEH have
been used largely for three sub-projects: microfilming
printed indexes of catalogues of Latin manuscript books;
compiling such indexes where they are lacking; collecting
unpublished catalogues of such manuscripts. These are at
various stages. The *Catalogus* has UAI sponsorship as well
as that of numerous societies and academies.

Index of Catalogues of Greek Manuscripts

Walter M. Hayes, c/o Dumbarton Oaks, 1703 32nd Street, NW,
    Washington, DC 20007

This project aims to produce an alphabetical finding list
of Greek authors and their works as preserved in manuscripts,
with detailed information on location and condition. It is
a joint venture of Dumbarton Oaks and the Pontifical
Institute of Medieval Studies, Toronto. The planned
end-product is a microfiche edition made from 3x5 inch index
cards. The project is scheduled for completion in 1981.

Manuel du latin chrétien

G. Sanders, Seminarie voor Postklassiek en Middeleeuws
    Latijn, Rijksuniversiteit Gent, Blandijnberg 2, 9000
    Gent, Belgium.

A new edition is in preparation of A. Blaise's work
(Strasbourg 1955); it will include a supplementary
bibliography of some 3,000 items.

Catalogues of Classical Manuscripts in France

L. Fossier, Institut de Recherche et d'Histoire des Textes,
    40 avenue d'Iéna, 75116 Paris, France

A supplement to volume II of M. Richard's *Catalogue des
manuscrits grecs* is in preparation, as is a catalogue of
Latin classical manuscripts kept in French public libraries.

Corpus Troporum

Leader: Ritva Jonsson, Särnavägen 7, 16142 Bromma, Sweden

The project aimed originally just to study tropes, the
elements which are added, as introductions or intercalations,
to the liturgy of the medieval western church. The
discovery of how much was unpublished or mispublished
turned the team's energies to a catalogue and publications
or republications. The catalogue (3 vols. to date) deals
only with the text, not the music. A fuller description
appears in *Journal of the Plainsong and Mediaeval Music
Society* 1 (1978) 98-115.

Inventory of Sequences 9th - 16th Centuries

Gordon A. Anderson, Dept. of Music, University of New
    England, Armidale, NSW, Australia 2351

In collaboration with Nancy van Deuren of the University
of Basel, Professor Anderson has collected since 1978 some
2,000 cards of melodies of sequences, representing some
400-500 melodies. Another four or five years are expected
to be needed for completing analysis of the collections,
and two further years to prepare a publication including
a thematic musical index.

BYZANTIUM

Dumbarton Oaks Bibliographies Based on Byzantinische Zeitschrift

Dumbarton Oaks, 1703 32nd Street NW, Washington, DC 20007
   (Director: Giles Constable)

Series I (Literature on Byzantine Art), already published, covers the period up to 1968; a ten-year supplement is in preparation. Series II (Literature on Various Byzantine Disciplines) will include literature through 1977; the first volume, *Epigraphy,* is expected to be published shortly. An Author Index is maintained at Dumbarton Oaks and a microform edition of it is planned.

Corpus Fontium Historiae Byzantinae

Dumbarton Oaks, 1703 32nd St. NW, Washington, DC 20007
   (Director: Giles Constable)

This series is proceeding with several subseries based in the centers involved: Berlin, Dumbarton Oaks, Brussels, Rome, Vienna, Thessaloniki. A list up to 1978 appears in the *Bulletin d'Information et de Coordination* 9 (1977/78) 24-26, published by the Association Internationale des Etudes Byzantines. Some 17 items are listed as published or in press, another 37 as in preparation.

Byzantine Greek Lexicon

Anastasius C. Bandy, Dept. of Literatures and Languages,
   University of California, Riverside, CA 92521

This lexicon is intended to cover the sixth to fifteenth centuries and to be an expansion of E.A. Sophocles' lexicon. Professor Bandy is at work on a canon of Byzantine authors

and titles and on collecting Latin loan words in Greek, but
any large-scale work is yet to begin.

Dictionary of Byzantium

Dumbarton Oaks, 1703 32nd St. NW, Washington, DC 20007
    (Director: Giles Constable)

This project, modeled on the Oxford Classical Dictionary,
is still in the planning stage. The proposed Board of
Editors includes Anthony Cutler, Nicholas Oikonomides,
Speros Vryonis, and Aleksander Kazhdan.

Traité d'études byzantines

Director: Paul Lemerle, 84 rue Vergniaud, 75013 Paris,
    France

Three volumes are currently in preparation: III, *Les
Manuscrits,* by a group headed by Jean Irigoin (Sorbonne);
Les Sceaux, by N. Oikonomides (Montreal); and VII, *Les
Monnaies,* by C. Morrisson (Paris).

Corpus of Dated Byzantine Inscriptions

Ihor Ševčenko and Cyril Mango, c/o Dumbarton Oaks, 1703
    32nd St. NW, Washington, DC 20007

The editors have been working actively during 1979/80 on
this project, and they hope for completion of Fascicle 1
in the near future.

ART AND ARCHAEOLOGY

Corpus Vasorum Antiquorum

Chairman, American Committee: Dietrich von Bothmer, Dept.
of Greek and Roman Art, Metropolitan Museum of Art,
Fifth Avenue at 82nd Street, New York, NY 10028

The *CVA*, begun in 1919, is a project of the Union
Académique Internationale. To date numerous fascicles have
been published in almost all countries where there are
collections of ancient vases; however the emphasis remains
Greek ceramics. In the U.S., work is currently underway on
a fascicle for the Smithsonian Institution.

Lexicon Iconographicum Mythologiae Classicae

Director of the U.S. Center: Jocelyn Penny Small, LIMC,
Language Building, Douglass College, Rutgers University,
New Brunswick, NJ 08903

The project embraces branches in thirty-five countries,
with a Central Editorial Office in Basel under the direction
of Lily Kahil. A multi-volume publication is planned, of
which the first volume is now in the press. The U.S. Center
is developing sophisticated computer software for the
creation of a data bank which will be available for
scholarly use.

Corpus Speculorum Etruscorum

Larissa Bonfante, Dept. of Classics, New York University,
25 Waverly Place, New York, NY 10003

The preparation of various fascicles for collections or
regions is in its early stage; an 8-person U.S. committee
headed by Professor Bonfante is organizing the project in

this country. An international committee is based on the
Istituto di Studi Etruschi ed Italici, Florence; a fascicle
for the Museo Civico of Bologna is the first scheduled for
publication.

ORIENTAL LANGUAGES

Coptic Encyclopedia

Editor in Chief: Aziz S. Atiya, 528 Marriott Library,
   University of Utah, Salt Lake City, UT 84112

The encyclopedia is still in the early stages: authors of
articles have been recruited and manuscripts have started
arriving.   The encyclopedia will treat all aspects of Coptic
civilization from language to archaeology.

Corpus dei Manoscritti Copti Letterari

Director: Tito Orlandi, Via Caroncini 19, 00197 Roma, Italy

This project aims to collect photographs of and data
concerning all Coptic literary manuscripts, and in
particular at the reconstruction of the White Monastery
library.   No single publication is envisaged, but many text
publications have appeared or are being prepared, and
several microfiche projects (photographs, bibliography,
etc.) are in the planning stages.

Graeco-Arabic Translation Literature

Dimitri Gutas, 321 Hall of Graduate Studies, Yale University,
   New Haven, CT 06520

This heading embraces a number of projects: an edition of
the Graeco-Arabic gnomologia; a *Glossarium Graeco-Arabicum*
for works translated into Arabic in the 8th-10th centuries;
an edition and study of Avicenna's commentaries on the works
of Aristotle; an edition of Arabic biographies and
bibliographies of Aristotle (other than Ptolemy's *Vita*).

61